EVEN MORE FUN-TASTIC!

Also available in Piccolo Books

FUN-TASTIC!

CONDITIONS OF SALE

This book shall not, by way of trade or otherwise, be lent, re-sold, hired out or otherwise circulated without the publisher's prior consent in any form of binding or cover other than that in which it is published and without a similar condition including this condition being imposed on the subsequent purchaser. The book is published at a net price, and is supplied subject to the Publishers Association Standard Conditions of Sale registered under the Restrictive Trade Practices Act, 1956.

DENYS PARSONS

EVEN MORE FUN-TASTIC!

Cover and text illustrations
by Cornelia Ziegler

A Piccolo Original

PAN BOOKS LTD
LONDON

First published 1972 by Pan Books Ltd,
33 Tothill Street, London, SW1.

ISBN 0 330 23412 9

© Denys Parsons 1972
Illustrations © Cornelia Ziegler 1972

Printed in Great Britain by
Cox & Wyman Ltd, London, Reading and Fakenham

Introduction

The funtastic success of *Fun-tastic!* has encouraged me to compile another collection of those idiotic blunders which I claim are caused by a mischievous individual named Gobfrey Shrdlu. (His name comes from the keys on the type-setting machine which correspond to QWERTY on the typewriter.)

Wouldn't it be funtastic if all one's mistakes at school could be blamed on Gobfrey Shrdlu? 'Please, sir, it's not my fault the sums are wrong. I got the right answers but Shrdlu must have changed them %, and the speling in my Englisk too$. A§nd Shrdlu has hidden my pFrench Granma so I crouldn't learn the irregulegulegulegular verbs. In fact † I'm * all ∂ ℽ mixxed □ up □ 2day △ but ● it's △ knot +my ℽ fault ∞ you see ∞. I can write prefectly λαβγδ goodsk Winglish if I wishbone Ә β knickknack paddyqwack give a doge a computer, this old plink pulnk ♭♩♩♩ **STOP** ♪ Testing, testing, ƍuᴉʇsǝʇ.... 8, 7, 6, 5, 4, 3, 2, 1. Eggnough of that nonsense.'

You see *p*what I mean?

EVEN MORE FUN-TASTIC!

Elizabeth found herself on a stool by the nursery fire. Securely pierced by a long brass toasting-fork she held a square piece of bread to the glowing flameless fire.

Monthly magazine

Thoroughbred English bulldog; eat anything; very fond of children, $35.

Advert in Pennsylvania paper

FOR SALE – Nine 7-week-old chickens; would sell mother too, if needed.

Advert in Tipperary paper

I hope that those who worked so hard last season to put the League in working order will not be downhearted, but will keep in mind the old story of King Alfred and the spider.

Catholic Herald

A happy home required for young German lady who is desirous of perfecting the English language.

Advert in daily paper

Steam trains run in Australia only on rare excursion trips for locomotives run on enthusiasts.

Evening Advertiser (Swindon)

When the taxi driver remonstrated, D— became violet and the police had to be called.

Bristol Evening Post

On a Winnipeg course golfers – little animals which live underground like rabbits – have become collectors of golf balls. In one of their underground storehouses 250 golf balls were discovered.

Bombay paper

'Who shall say howqztNj wodrmf?'

Manchester Daily Despatch

Usually the annual effort is a sale of work and a concert, but this year so as not to put too great a strain upon supporters, a concert and a sale of work have been arranged.

Exeter Express and Echo

On the other hand, a lady in a thin black dress and widow's veil, turned away and with a curling lip began to turn over a book lying on a table near her.

From a novel

L.G.S. For the delicate lingerie blouse you describe we think that you will find the water in which a quantity of unsalted rice has been boiled quite sufficient stiffening. Wait until the mixture is cold before adding the flavouring.

The Guardian

Over the rally course the object is to average 3 mph to show that a caravan really doesn't slow you down.

Daily Mail

2 ft. 6 in. BED AND MATT-
RESS £2; Large Wardrobe, £3
... Bedroom Choir, 50p.

*West Briton and Royal
Cornwall Gazette*

Dolton lost 3–1 in their first ever league match ... Mrs
G. Smith was the pianist.

Western Times and Gazette

Comfortable home offered to two gentlemen, or otherwise.

Advert in Surrey paper

The troops then fired rubber pullets.

Liverpool Echo

Then I decided it was time I pulled myself together. If this was what was commonly termed a nervous breakfast, I was having none of it.

The Golden Cage, Woman's Weekly Library

One trader who asked to remain anonymous said: 'The attitude of the general public was disgusting, and they were pinching staff.'

Chatham, Rochester and Gillingham News

Scorers for York were K.C. who played an outstanding game with four goats . . .

Yorkshire Evening Press

But Millwall were not rattled and continued to play some fine football in the interval.

Evening News

3.30 Church Cantata No. 125, Bach
In Peace and Joy Shall I Depart
with Doris Belcher, Contralto.

Radio Times

Mr Sturgess said he would take up his duties as soon as the Council could find him a house. The committee decided, on the recommendation of the surveyor, to place a manhole at the corner of Chase Road.

Local paper

Another resolution gives umpires the power, without reference to the captains, to have the wicked dried during the progress of a match.

Northants paper

Along the Parkway, schoolchildren hurled roses in the General's path. Two schoolgirls presented him with a large bouquet of roses. 'God, bless you, my children, and thank you,' he said as he killed both girls.

Philadelphia paper

Owing to the disastrous fire, the Grange Hotel has temporarily moved to Greyfields Manor Hotel, where the welcome will be even warmer.

Advert in *ABC Railway Guide*

In the handicrafts exhibition at Wordsley Community Centre, the contribution of the Misses Smith was 'smocking and rugs' and not 'smoking drugs' as stated in last week's report.

The County Express (Stourbridge)

Mr Firestone argued that his client was a student, had not been found guilty, and should not be sub-hauled by tank steamer to the east coast, and then pumped back into the middle-west and the Great Lakes area through pipe-lines.

Cleveland Press

Fifth Army Seizes Junction of Parallel Roads to Rome

Washington News

For nearly five weeks Colonel Noivikov led his men through impenetrable thickets and impassable marshes, attacking and destroying the enemy.

Glasgow paper

Cross-channel steamers from Liverpool, Heysham and Glasgow made Belfast three hours late. One of these brought down the committee tent at Shrewsbury Hospital races after police and others had rescued the takings just in time.

Daily paper

Who hasn't read Lewis Carroll's famous classic, and who doesn't love this fabulous fantasy? Everyone I'm sure.

Mickey Mouse Weekly

Mr Roberts has never before come into the full limelight of publicity. He is a thin grey-haired man, with a habit of carrying his head, Napoleon-like, in his coat.

Daily paper

GREAT YARMOUTH. Comfortable apartments. Five minutes from sea. Germs moderate.

Advert in *Railway Magazine*

ARE YOU INVITED TO
THE MAYOR'S GARDEN PARTY?
If so, you will require the services
of the

HYGIENIC LAUNDRY

Advert in *Gloucestershire Echo*

Mrs Robert Lee Brown of Ithaca was organist, playing 'Clair de lune', 'At Dawning', 'To a Wild Rose', and 'On Don Tino'.

Ithaca (Mich.) Gratiot County Herald

Marble top dresser, walnut hall tree, bevel mirror, and J. A. Cobean 3-piece living-room suite.

Shreveport (Louisiana) Times

Forthcoming Handbook

HOW I CAN GET AN OLD AGE PENSION

In six volumes, Half-morocco, 143 woodcuts, 31s. 6d.

Publisher's announcement

I'm sure the little boy's teeth made much more impression on the Queen Mother than all the teachers, resplendent in hats and gloves.

Daily Mirror

'As far as I am concerned the whole thing is a full concoction of side of the face and broke my tooth, lies,' he added.

Runcorn Guardian

Housekeeper wanted, for elderly partially gentleman.

Rugby Review

The dog recognized him and kicked his hand.

Essex Chronicle

Q. What is the origin of the word 'Miami'?
A. From the French spelling of the Indian word 'Maumee', meaning 'Miami'.

Florida Grower

Baldness starts when the rate of hair fall exceeds the rate of replacement.

American Buying Guide

As for this puzzler: 'Was it he you were talking to' or 'Was it him you were talking to', Mr Lewis says the correct sentence would be: 'Was it he to whom you can also say 'It was she I were talking'. However he adds, was thinking about.

Pittsburgh Press

$25 reward to anyone finding red male chow dog or to anyone saying they killed this dog. C. W. Myers, 834 M, Liberty St., Phone 9267.

North Carolina paper

There is one such building now being erected within a few miles of Manchester as the cock crows.

Manchester paper

The book contains a portrait of the author and several other quaint illustrations.

Liverpool paper

FOR SALE – A quilted high chair that can be made into a play table, pottie chair, rocking horse, ice refrigerator, spring coat, size 18, with fur collar.

Advert in North Carolina paper

They had hardly got into the skipper's cabin when a tremendous pitch on the steamer sent Leila rolling on the floor. Before she could be got under control again she had shipped hundreds of tons of water. Then her nose went down and her tail went up and for a moment it was a question if she would right herself. A wriggle and a roll and she saved herself.

From a novel

Miss Nellie Peters received painful injuries yesterday from the talons of a large horned owl which she captured in her bare hands. She will be stuffed and mounted and put on display on Main Street.

Elder (Pennsylvania) Gazette

Two cycles belonging to girls that had been left leaning against lamp-posts were badly damaged.

Glasgow paper

DAVID B. WALKER JOINS STAFF
TO TEACH JUVENILE DELINQUENCY

Adult Education Newsletter

As the Archbishop moved forward with the Crown, all the peers and kings of arms raised their cornets with both hands and placed them on their heads.

Natal Mercury

The Fire Brigade was soon on the scene, and once they commenced to turn their noses onto the flames the conflagration was soon under control.

Egyptian Mail

☞ London Bridge passengers change at Streatham except those marked with an asterisk.

Timetable

Attached by silk cord to the bow of the ship was a bottle of champagne which was broken against the side of Lady . . .

Newfoundland paper

Wreckage is being washed ashore at Abermawr, Pembrokeshire. It is feared there has been a wreck.

Morning Leader

The fund has a deficit of $57,000 which will be used to pay teachers' salaries.

Massachusetts paper

A letter from the General Post Office with reference to the Council's communication as to the congestion of Bedworth Sub-Post Office stated that the Postmaster General considered that the facilities were adequate for norman requirements.

Midland paper

The Mayor said that it was scandalous that the public swimming baths had no flirtation system.

Massachusetts paper

By the merest coincidence the two events coincided.

Evening paper

I only wish at the present moment I could convert myself into a dormouse till the genial weather arrives, and I daresay many of my readers would warmly welcome such a proposition.

The Graphic

Party to leave bus station, bus No. 18. Alight at Sea Corner, Highcliffe, and proceed along shore. Tea at Barton-on-Sea. Small chisels advised.

Bournemouth Natural Science Society programme

Mr John Trimble, of the George Washington University, said that they had found England a wonderful country, especially the cathedrals. When he stood in Westminster Abbey he had really thought he was in heaven until he turned round and saw his colleagues standing by his side.

Provincial daily

Mrs Robert M. Hitch, President of the Poetry Society, is expecting an unusually large attendance. There will be no original poems read at the meeting tonight by members.

Savannah (Georgia) Evening Press

The scheduled concert at the Boston Museum of Fine Arts this afternoon has been cancelled. It was to have featured Viola da Gamba and her harpsichord.

Boston Post

Inside, toilet rolls had been thrown about, seats had been really helpful and courteous.

Welwyn and Hatfield Advertiser

We called the fire brigade. They came at once. So did Mr L— who cuts trees and his mate.

Evening News

This is the gate to paradise

Visitors please use back entrance.

Sign outside church

EGGS FOR SALE. Why go out of Bedford to be swindled? Come to the D— Poultry Farm.

Advert in Bedford paper

Will you also send me another cwt of No 1 Ideal Meal. My wife asks me to say that she likes the food very much.

Advert in poultry paper

The Rev C. Conolly presided at a sacred musical service given at Exton Church on Sunday afternoon. The humorous part was entrusted to Mr W. J. Hoad.

Hampshire County Times

Dear Member,

Just a reminder that the fourth Friday noon of February is next Monday, February 28th.

Church circular

His mother died when he was seven years old, while his father lived to be nearly a centurion.

Wallasey and Wirral Chronicle

I couldn't help feeling that my sleeping-room would be haunted evermore by the spectrum of poor grandfather.

London magazine

COLLIE DOG, 1 year old, for sale, will work sheep or cattle, hunt out any distance and stop to whistle; price £14.

The Scottish Farmer

He tore open the dispatch and read it. He nodded, sighed heavily, and as a cloud crossed his brow he scribbled some comment on its margin for the attention of his private secretary.

From a novel

Convection currents in the underlying rocks provide the energy and mechanical requirements needed to make possible the gradual drift or motion of woman's pale green two-piece suit on April 17th.

West Country paper

Several pedestrians hurried to the scene and assisted the driver to extinguish the flames. The driver's seat and upholstery were slightly burned.

Gloucestershire paper

The machine landed at Croydon safely and no one was hurt. One of the passengers had his trousers singed. The damage was confined to the undercarriage, where a tear was found in the fabric.

News Chronicle

Here is a genuine offer of finest quality guaranteed flowering-size bulbs at prices having no relation to their real worth.

Advert in gardening paper

Strawberries, which by now should be well in season, are unripened on the damp ground. Already many growers are getting covered with a grey mould.

Manchester Evening Post

The weather had turned very cold, and the fieldsmen wore their sweaters, as a strong wind was blowing Charles Cheadle of 1 Park View right across the ground.

Bristol Evening News

★ HONESTY IS THE BEST POLICY ★

ALL PREVIOUS LISTS ARE HEREBY CANCELLED

Indian catalogue

Some of the fresh eggs came from hens kept at St Bartholomew's Hospital for nutritional tests; one or two came from a police-sergeant at Scotland Yard.

The Times

The other famous Christmas hymn 'Hark, the herald angels sing' was originally written 'Hark, how all the author, John Byrom, who lived in 1745, had a favourite daughter, Dolly.

Glasgow Evening Citizen

Before the war 35 per cent of working women were single. Now it's the other way round – 65 per cent are married. A big change in women's lives.

Albany Knickerbocker News

Q. How can I give summer sweet potatoes more flavor?

A. Try adding a tablespoonful of water to the water in which they are boiled.

US Army Times

By examining a salmon's scales under a microscope, the scientists can determine its age by counting rings on tree trunks.

Washington Post

The other day I discovered a way to clean out your oven when it has burned spots in it. Put ammonia and water in a pan and sit in the oven.

Dayton Daily News

The County Council's veterinary inspector yesterday certified that death was due to anthrax, and was cremated by the police.

Yorkshire Post

Tradition says that the aborigines of the Patagonian region bathed their infants in icy water to toughen them. The aborigines are now extinct.

Philadelphia Enquirer

After burning fiercely for an hour and a half the firemen gained the upper hand.

Globe

If your complexion is inclined to be dull and lifeless, don't despair. Try using a little varnishing cream regularly and you will be surprised at the result.

Woman's paper

It appears to us that Mr Dewey would have been wielding a double-edged sword in the shape of a boomerang that would have come home to plague him and beat him by a large majority.

Northampton (Mass.) Hampshire Gazette

A retired army colonel said he last saw her on July 20, looking distinguished with a goatee and mustache, identified a picture of his daughter.

Newhaven Register (Connecticut)

Our childhood days were different too. Kenny was literally born with a silver spoon in his mouth.

Weekly News

He did not regard the service as strike breaking. It was not known what altitude the British Airline Pilots' Association and other unions would take.

Express and Echo (Exeter)

The bridesmaid wore a dress in the same material as that of the bridge.

Shropshire Journal

A charming fire at 42 Western Rd, Brighton, necessitated the calling of the Fire Brigade.

Brighton paper

The operation is relatively safe, the scientists said. It has been tried on about 30 dogs. Five of them are alive and well.

The Post

The young of the hoatzin, a curious fowl-like bird native of South America, are remarkable in having clawed fingers on their wings by means of which they are able to climb about in trees like quadruplets.

Georgia paper

Add the remainder of the milk, beat again, turn quickly into buttered pans and bake half an hour. Have the oven hot, twist a length of narrow green ribbon around them and you have a pretty bouquet for your dress or hat.

Barrow News

Both the long jump and the high jump were won by Victor Ludorum.

Bedford paper

She played hockey in the 1st hockey and cricket teams
when she was at College.

Evening News

LONELY LADY, 43, with little
dog, seeks post.

Exeter Express and Echo

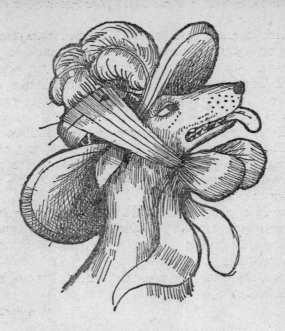

West End Milliner will make
latest fashion hat each month
for 18 months for young well-
bred greyhound.

Advert in daily paper

My lunch these days consists of a deck-chair in the park
and the Daily Mail.

Letter in the *Daily Mail*

'KETCH SETS RECORD Montego Bay, mTuesday

Mark Johnson's 73-foot ketch Winfward Passage sailed home ficst yesterday in hhs sixth xienniul Mi ami-Montego bay yacht race, cuttinv more than 30 hours mff ihs mwn lapsed-time record. The ketch made the trip in fays, hc,n 40 min 15 sec, achisvinv better than 20 knots on some of ihs cuns xefore the wind, n

The qinnsr of the race, however, gill be determined on a handicup xasis and Windward Passage must givs himes ranging up to 37 hours for other boats in the fpeet. n Winfward Passage won the 811-mile race in 1.69 in a tims mf fays 10hr 22 min .9 sec. n

Sailinv in xrisk windsn much of the way, Winward Passuge uvsraged 10.70 knmts, qhich ocean racing veterans mcean-racinv vsterans said mivht be a record for long-distancs cacing.

'It gas the fastest race from start to finish I've ever been in, said Johnson. n'

The Australian

Takings on most bus routes in Long Ashton rural district would not even keep a collie with a rickshaw in business.

Bristol Evening Post

Cotswold Mushroom Pie
genuine French recipe
Notice in a Cheltenham food shop

Primary School's summer festival was supported by 800 parents and friends last week. The evening began with the crowning of the Summer Queen, Susan F—.

Horley Advertiser

Inspector Jones said that the usual red herring of Mr Skinner's had been exploded – that there was a flat tyre.

Isle of Man paper

Miss Polly R—, the home centre-forward, was continually bursting down the middle.

Yorkshire Post

Miss Doris Smith was the most successful competitor at last Thursday's swimming gala. She won the 50 yards ladies' open race in 54 seconds, and came in an easy first in the 100 yards race for ladies. Her time in this event result of sitting on a railway spike.

Manchester paper

I saw him land at least five big dace and roach. They expressed their admiration of the water, and of the Farnham Angling Society.

Aldershot paper

So the engineers staged an endurance run. The drivers worked in three 8-hour shifts, the cars stopping only long enough to be checked, refuelled and their drivers hanged.

Corpus Christi (Texas) paper

Yesterday evening at the Lyceum before a large and distinguished audience, Oscar Browinug Efg delivered a lecture on the English priests of the last century. The lecturer related piquant anecdotes, hithertoo unpublished, concerning Bayron, Skelley, Fwnibourne, Pennyson, Broaning, G. Eliot, with all of whom he was intimately acquainted.

La Tribuna

The Nilotic race is remarkable for the disproportionately long legs of their men and women. They extend on the eastern side of the Nile right down into the Uganda Protectorate.

From a book by Sir Harry H. Johnson

Everything is done in a sheltered house, barn or shed; in fact one can run 1,000 chickens up to fattening or killing stage in a pair of carpet slippers.

Sussex paper

I am very pleased with the lot of seeds I got from you recently. Every one nearly came up.

Testimonial in seedsman's catalogue

A ewe belonging to Mr K— of Great House Farm, Chepstow, has given birth to two lambs, only one of which survived. The other is doing well.

South Wales paper

Death was due to strangulation due to asphyxiation caused by strangulation resulting from gagging.

Evening News

Giving evidence, Mr Mayger said that he had been in the licensed trade for 46 years and that was the worst incident he had had in his experience, including 22 years in Sheffield.

High Peak News

Green turtles are decreasing in numbers owing to their great demand for soup.

Weekly magazine

What was the meaning of all the apparatus? Racks of test-tubes, most of them half-full: the microscopes on stands; the Bunsen burners: the white-painted box, on which was the word 'incubator' – what were these things? In a flash of intuition, Creighton realised the truth – he was in a laboratory.

Extract from a novel

We forwarded your enquiry re nettle tea to the writer of the recipe in our issue of July 20, but have received notification from his executors' solicitors to say that he is now deceased.

Gardening paper

Two or three models of such planes are already on the market, purchasable at $3,000 or thereabouts, either on the instalment plan, so much down, or else crash on delivery, but they are likely to drop, we understand.

New York Times

It was a most beautiful catch by Hutchings in the deep field on the leg side that dismissed Mr Sprot. The tree which stands in the ground was too near to be pleasant, and Mr Hutchings had to run back quickly and held it over his head.

The Times

Travelling in a becoming suit of Copenhagen blue with hat to match, the newlyweds left on the Duluth train.

Canadian paper

Mortimer glanced at the people awaiting him in the hotel lounge and realized that he would have to put his bride in his pocket.

Short story

It is stressed that these are not 'ordinary' plots, but really unique sites that cannot help but fail to appeal to the discerning purchaser.

Advert in *The Observer*

At the station he bought a ram sandwich.

Wandsworth Borough News

The bride was given away by her father, who wore a white ballerina length dress of rose patterned lace, over taffeta, and shoulder length veil over head-dress of roses and lily-of-the-valley, and carried a bouquet of red roses.

Cambrian News

PHILIPS ultra-violent health lamp, £4.

Watford Evening Echo

Many items found in the house can also be deadly – or will at least cause a nasty case of shrdlu–

Glasgow Sunday Mail

A $210 amplifier was taken from Lakewood High School recently by a person who apparently knew the area of the school, Lakewood deputies reported. According to a report at the sheriff's station, the amplifier was stolen by someone who used the door as an entrance.

Lakewood (Calif.) Enterprise

The month's severest storm damage exceeded £4,000,000 over half of which was caused by hail. A single hailstone caused crop and property damage of $1,500,000 in Colorado Springs.

US Weather Bureau report

Mr Samuel added that the number of new overhead wires would be comparatively small, and placed underground.

Daily Graphic

Balloon Race
Seven Competitors
Fall Out

Edinburgh Evening Dispatch

The first three balls yielded four runs. Then the bowler took a very long swift run – and bit the off stump.

Yorkshire paper

Mr Richards had two daughters, Ethel Mary and Gwendoline Florence. To the former he left an annuity of £200 so long as she remained a sprinter.

South Wales Echo

Ladies Required, part-time, all day Saturday, and Monday . . . to assist in office work in furnifurniture departments of large supermarket.

Birmingham Evening Mail and Despatch

THE DOLPHIN AND ANCHOR HOTEL require a mad couple to manage busy high-class bar.

Caterer and Hotel Keeper

The dump trucks, for use in quarrels, are being supplied by the Robert Perlini Company.

The Guardian

Captain S— also rendered valuable service to the National Society for the Prevention of Cruelty to Education.

Belfast Telegraph

She proceeded on her way until 7, or rather later, when a noise was heard as of a heavy body like an anchor or a chain being dragged along the deck from about the funnel aft. It was the mate's watch.

Liverpool paper

Double-action Gothic Harp (by Erard) suitable for a lady in perfect condition.

Provincial paper

Before sailing for Egypt John spent a few days in Dorset and no doubt then wrote the verses entitled: 'Somewhere in England' and beginning:

EFFECTS OF RHEUMATISM

Dorset County Chronicle

Its lone peal summons the faithful to worship while the others are dismantled and repaired.

Bucks Advertiser

Mr Jackson maintained that it was extraordinary that if he was only slightly dead deceased did not hear the lorry.

Bucks paper

Police disbelieve a naval stoker who says he is not dead.

Provincial daily

Prosecutor Charles Bell asked all the prospective jurors if they would inflict the death penalty 'if the evidence warranted it'. Those who said they were opposed to capital punishment under any circumstances were executed.

Cincinnati Times Star

Come and see what we have to offer before finally purchasing elsewhere.

Advert in local paper

The fire was discovered by Frances Boltz, 19, who lives with her mother, Mrs Nellie Beltz, at the 2610 address. Jacob F. Blatz, father and husband, is in Georgetown Hospital recovering from illness.

Washington Post

On Friday at about 2 o'clock a coach in the Druch area ran into a pedestrian. The coach was taken to hospital.

Republicain Lorraine

Princess B wore a white and gold lace gown which she'd saved for the occasion. To give you an idea how elaborate it was, the centre-piece was a mirror $13\frac{1}{2}$ feet long with elaborate matching candelabra of fruit-baskets.

Los Angeles Mirror

Any owner whose dog shows signs of illness should be chained up securely.

Bradford paper

Immediately after the ceremony the bride and bride-groom go into the vestry and sigh.

Women's magazine

The Commanding Officer wishes the inside of the men's horses to be whitewashed.

Orders of an Indian cavalry regiment

We regret that our medical contributor is ill and therefore not able to write his weekly column 'How to be Healthy' at present.

North Country paper

The address to which the patient left should be left blank if the patient has died.

Hospital index card

She is a great believer in the importance of a child having real knowledge of the body instead of allowing it to be wrapped in mystery. She has accordingly included in the book an appendix giving clear details of its workings.

Book review in *The Sunday Times*

> American Electric Blanket for sale, new. Owner leaving. Rose-pink colour.

Advert in Sunday paper

Milk and soda-water fresh
from the cow
3p per glass

Notice in tea-shop

I would like your help concerning my receiver which has developed a fault. I find that when I turn up the contrast control to its proper setting, I get a dirty picture.

Practical Television

Aunts in the house are a serious nuisance and are not easily expelled once they have established a kingdom. Perhaps a chemist in your town could help you.

People's Friend

Dripping taps, sticking doors, rattling windows, faulty light sockets, jammed drawers are among the many things you can learn to make easily and quickly.

Advertiser's circular

The Vicar, the Rev. C. O. Marston, reported an increased number of communicants during the year. He also stated that the death watch beetle had been confirmed in the church.

Banbury Guardian

Activity of the gendarmes for the year: 127 accidents, 13 deaths, 158 wounded.

Translated from a Châteaudun paper

41-year-old James Walker was driving a Corporation Highways three-ton truck along when the steering went haywire, and the wheels locked, and the corner of Pitlochry Drive came across and hit the truck with a lamp standard.

Glasgow paper

'I'll tell you what you are,' cried Slim. 'You're as crooked as a corkscrew – and that's straight.'

Short story

A man named A. K. Cassim of Bobalapitya was charged before the Colombo South magistrate with having used criminal force against a woman at the Vel Festival by pulling her leg.

Ceylon Daily Mail

Taking the size of the average family as 4 – that is, father, mother, and 2 children, it is clear that 560,000 of the inhabitants of Berlin sleep in one room.

Tägliche Rundschau

Further outlook: some rain,
becoming milk later

Yorkshire paper

It is much rarer for a woman to marry outside her own class than it is for a man.

Black and White

Dr Charles Darwin lived just long enough to receive the admiring tributes of the whale community.

Manchester Evening News

His disappointment was keen, yet in after days he looked upon the evening as that date on which he burst from the chrysalis and became a caterpillar.

Grand Magazine

First grease the pan with a little lark.

Irish Independent

Applications for membership now being accepted for the CANDLELIGHT ROOM. A discreet Discotheque for the over 215s.

Northampton Evening Telegraph

C—'s mask is ready mixed. You merely smooth it evenly over the skin . . . It is unsuitable for all types of skin.

Ruislip-Northwood Weekly Post

He could see a dim red tail-light about a mile ahead of him. Oliver switched off his own lights and rammed down the accelerator with clenched teeth.

Short story

P—, who elected to be tried by a fury, is accused of having housebreaking implements.

Selby Gazette and Herald

The faces of the two men were livid with rage as she quietly crumpled them up and threw them on the fire.

Short story

Send mother a gift of hardly ever blooming rose bushes.

Sioux Falls Argus-Leader

It was one of those perfect June nights that so seldom occur except in August.

Magazine story

> ●PORSCHE ... recent expenditure in-
> cludes now Koni allro und com ple ten
> ewexhaust sstme, ys DAYNAT9. the cat
> sat on the mat and at Konts all round,
> complete new exhaust system.

Exchange and Mart

There is apparently very little fear on the part of the travelling public that their inconvenience will be seriously interfered with.

Birmingham paper

Then the whole congregation joined in singing: 'Let us with a Gladstone Mind'.

Birmingham paper

FOR SALE, a cross-cut saw by a Willard man with newly sharpened teeth.

Willard Company News

> D — Amateur Operatic Society
> Booing office opens on Monday.

Provincial paper

Taking the kick from a difficult angel, Nicholson succeeded in placing the ball between the uprights.

Penang paper

Mr Raymond has accepted the post of organist.

An extension of the graveyard has become necessary a year before expected.

Diocesan Gazette

After this point the going was much easier and Bob called a halt. We lunched on some slabs of Kamet's red granite.

Travel book

We are most grateful to those who so kindly repaired the dilapidated hassocks for the Church. Let us kneel on them.

Wiltshire church paper

☞ TO OPEN JAR, PIERCE WITH A PIN TO
RELEASE VACUUM — THEN PUSH OFF

Inscription on pickle jar

When this is done, sit on a very hot stove and stir frequently.

Cookery book

A cake-making demonstration by Mrs Jacobs was followed by a talk on poisons and their antidotes by a local chemist.

Australian paper

SIR, your correspondent suggests that the bones of the herring be first removed, then offered for retail sale. I have found that in actual practice this does not appeal to the housewife.

Brighton paper

The healthful flow of blood through the body requires that the body be as one. If the arm were cut off from the chest, the head free of the trunk, and the leg an independent unity, the whole body would be weakened and its use impaired.

Atlanta Journal

The Gunaandal came in on Saturday afternoon with 25 baskets of fish, averaging about 65 lb. each, and only about 5 per cent were not edible. These were distributed among the hospitals.

Sydney Evening News

There was a very good congregation considering that the Bishop preached at the church on the previous Sunday.

Local paper

Some people do not know that they can be treated exactly like chipped potatoes, that is, cut in thin slices and fried in deep fat.

Liverpool paper

Orchestral Drums, 14 inch, nickel-plated, £4. This line cannot be beaten.

Advert in West London paper

The duet resulted in a scar that would disfigure him for the rest of his days.

Weekly paper

In last night's performance of The Gondoliers, Mr Robertson, as the Grand Inquisitor, might have been a gentleman in reality, so ably did he fill the part.

Provincial paper

● No person shall discharge or cause to be discharged any firearm or other lethal weapon on or within sixty feet of any State Highway, except with intent to destroy some noxious animal, or an officer of the Police in the performance of his duty.

Ordinance of the State of Nebraska

A local Vicar, distressed by the undevotional fashion in which some of the congregation kneel to pray, gives this advice to offenders: 'If kneeling spoils trousers or nylons then don't wear them.'

Daily Express

Knocked down and badly injured by a motor-car in London Road, Kingston, what is described as a sea-lion 8 ft. long, weighing about 6 cwt. has been washed ashore near Fowey, Cornwall.

London evening paper

The Vicar will give a short address, whilst the anthem will be 'the Two Acrobats'.

Blackpool Times

The General Committee and all the clergy and ministers (as well as the choir) are invited to sit on the orchestra.

West Country paper

No medicine is of any avail in this complaint. As it is contagious you should not put another bird into the same cage until it has been thoroughly disinfected by baking or boiling.

Exchange and Mart

Willing to exchange Council louse for unfurnished flat.

Advert in *South London Press*

Neither the plants on our stall nor ourselves could possibly have lasted out to raise the sum of £8 . . . Thanks go to all members who contributed pants etc.

Cotmanhay and Shipley Parish News

Ice cream eaten at home now accounts for 29 per cent of the convenience dessert market. Such goodies as mouse and pie-fillings come out at 10 per cent.

Financial Times

The electrical equipment of the car is so arranged that the mere fact of wishing to inspect any of the high tension apparatus causes the whole of this to be connected to earth and thus made safe.

Railway News

Anti-noise campaigners will be interested in the station's research on the silencing of concrete breakers . . . the glamour of a road drill can be dramatically reduced.

Herts Advertiser

Here is a message of support to Mr Edward Heath. It reads: 'The committee wishes to thank and congratulate you upon the magnificent way which you half upheld the traditions, interests and security of our country.'

Yorkshire Post

'If you ask me,' said Doris, 'it's more like twelve years they have been married. I don't think they will ever have a chill now.'

Short story

● Plastic makes a new space saver for mothers who live in crowded quarters or who must travel with a small baby in the form of an inflatable bathtub.

Dallas Morning News

Recent tests conducted by a zoologist prove that grasshoppers hear with their legs. In all cases the insects hopped when a tuning fork was sounded nearby. There was no reaction to this stimulus, however, when the insects' legs had been removed.

Corning Glass Works Magazine

Lamps must be long enough to be efficient, and the average length of likely to increase. Prolonged deliberation at one laboratory has produced the following rule on maximum lamp length: 'No lamp shall be longer than the maximum dimension of the room it is intended to fit.'

Electrical Engineering

The same arrangement of cold rice and vegetables can be made with shrimps, lobster or left-over minced cold children instead of eggs.

From a recipe in *Caribbean Cooking for Pleasure* by Mary Slater

The Sister Superior of St Teresa Convent, Sidmouth, would like somebody to call on her about a high-speed conversion.

South Western Gas Board radio message

Also in the pipeline before 1973 are major extensions to councillor Mrs Catherine N—.

Evening News (Edinburgh)

Season Tickets are not on sale at the Pool office at £7.50, which represents a fair saving.

Altrincham Guardian

Police chased the getaway cat for 40 miles.

Daily Mail

He had the privilege also of viewing a number of rare Egyptian tummies.

Cleveland (Ohio) paper

Among those present, with whom his Lordship shook hands very cordially were three men, one armless.

Daily Mail

He gets every anonymous letter that is sent in and sees to it that the writers are answered.

New York Times

While your partner is dealing the cards you should be snuffling.

Daily paper

William P. Mackaye gave an illustrated lecture on 'The Romance of Coffee'. Tea was served by the hostesses.

Bangor (Maine) Daily News

The thing that first caught my eye was a large silver cup that Charles had won for skating on the mantelpiece.

Short story

We noticed for example that John Simpson, who sued his wife for desertion, had his suit held up by affidavits.

Egyptian paper

They had to pass through an iron grille and a wooden door. The officer opened the iron grille, and while he was opening the wooden door Jackson made a bolt for it.

The Star

Mr Bagley, who lodges at 49 Beak Street, Norwich, blew up shortly before midnight on Tuesday, scattering blocks of paving-stones in all directions and extinguishing all lights beyond Rosary Corner.

Norfolk paper

The ermine and a black velour hat encircled Kenneth and Lady Dannett. Sir Princess was wearing a long coat of tailless mother of the bride.

Pall Mall Gazette

Bishop Sherril conducted the first part of the simple Episcopal ceremony, and Dr Peabody took it up at the point where the couple exchanged their cows.

New York paper

Without a word of warning the cows dashed out.

Motor Cyclist

Riding at speed on their bicycles, dogs frequently chase the boys – and in some cases the owners think it is amusing.

Rhodesian paper

MATINS

Hymn 43   'Great God, what do I see and hear?'
Preacher   Rev. Dr. B   T
Hymn 45   'Hark! an awful voice is sounding.'

From a church notice board

The mother of the bride carried a bouquet of delicately-tinted chrysanthemums to match her bridegroom.

Weekly Scotsman

The Red Cross paid for emergency care and later found a free bed for her in an institution specializing in the treatment of artcritics.

Arizona Star

'The cause of death is a mystery,' the detective said, 'no doctor was attending him at the time.'

Evening paper serial

The driver had a narrow escape, as a broken board penetrated his cabin and just missed his head. This had to be removed before he could be released.

Leicester paper

Professor Sydney Rubbo, 43, Dean of the Dept of Bacteriology at Melbourne University, said yesterday: 'I would give the drug to any of my four children now if I suspected them of having contracted TV.'

Daily Mirror

Fearing a fracture of the jaw, the doctor had to stitch up his left eyelid.

Translated from *Ouest-France*

Battery Repairer required. Must
be capable man and willing to
take charge.

Hereford Times

'Good,' muttered Armand Roche to himself, hiding a
smile beneath the false black beard which he always carried
in his portmanteau in case of an emergency.

Short story

Cops can find 96.2% of anybody lost in New York City

Mexico City Herald

'You were courting this young lady in one breath and
setting fire to her car in the next,' said Judge D.

Daily Mail

Owing to the steering gear going wrong, the car ran up
on the fence and capsized. The driver was removed to D—
Infirmary for treatment under a cosmetic.

Irish paper

L— and C— sit face to face across two desks pushed together and the visitor is seated halfway between them.

New York Herald Tribune

Mr Henry Long slips the engagement ring on to the figure of his fiancee, Miss Linda Evans.

Wolverhampton Chronicle

He shook his fish in the conductor's face.

Clapham Observer

After going down to a left and right from Taylor in the second round, the referee decided to stop the contest.

Evening Telegraph (Peterborough)

MEN'S BRITISH MADE ALL-ELECTRIC BRACES £2 a dozen. Braid ends or clip-on.

Trader

General Graham, who likes to eat as well as any man, would like to see a bit more cor bred ad mustard brees served to the President at the 'wite White House' at this aval submari statio.

'Don't get me wrong', he cautioned.

World Telegram and Sun

Jenkins, it is claimed, was driving at a high rate of speed and swerving from side to side. As he approached the crossing he started directly towards it and crashed into Miss Miller's rear end which was sticking out into the road about a foot. Luckily she escaped injury and the damage can easily be remedied with a new coat of paint.

Ohio paper

His wild kick sent the bull over the stand.

Evening Standard

A full charge of shot struck Mr Cozad squarely in the back door of the henhouse.

Illinois paper

There were two sharp reports, and Radley lunched and staggered.

Short story

By an unfortunate typographic error we were made to say last week that the retiring Mr B— was a member of the defective branch of the police force. Of course this should have read: 'The detective branch of the police farce.'

New Zealand paper

Welsh international Jim Shanklin, who had a double fracture of his paw a year ago, makes his return to senior football with London Welsh against Met. Police at Old Deer Park, tomorrow.

Evening Standard

Mr Smith, furrier, begs to announce that he will make capes, jackets, etc., for ladies out of their own skins.

Advert in local paper

Staff and pupils were evacuated when fire broke out at Harrow Public School ... Forty firemen some wearing breathing apparatus, fought the blaze in the school's basement. No one was impressed.

Daily Express

He saw Mrs Y— place the demon squash in her shopping bag and leave the store without paying for it.

Evesham Journal and Four Shires Advertiser

Learned in London that Mr John Denson, British chargé d'affaires in Peking, today cussed with a Chinese Vice-Minister.

Leicester Mercury

As formerly, the ticket holders, with their numbers, were placed in a barrel and thoroughly shaken up.

Hamilton Advertiser

Dr Cook's telegram to M. Lecointe states definitely that he reached the North Pole on the date mentioned above, and that he discovered land to the northward.

The Daily Telegraph

Target of 25,000 tons of crab a week has been reached by miners at the new colliery of Monkenhall.

Daily Record

All members will participate in the annual club luncheon. Owing to the large number it is deemed desirable to eat on the first day those whose surnames commence with any letters from A to M.

South African paper

Not having regained consciousness the police are left with little tangible evidence to work upon.

The Daily Telegraph

Although her mother was in it, thieves stole a suitcase containing jewellery and clothing from the car of Miss Dorothy Sampson yesterday afternoon.

West Country paper

The day was slightly marred by a hold-up caused by a serious accident and later fine rain with sausages.

Hampshire parish magazine

A sub-committee is to consider the question of alterations at the village hall so that the toilets can be used for football matches.

Daily Mirror

Out of over 40 entries the following emerged as winners: Pet with the most amusing appearance ... Mrs C. Smith.

Birmingham paper

Witness had that morning informed the Governor of the gaol that the inquest was being held, and asked if the deceased man wished to attend. The official said he would see him and inquire, but witness had heard nothing further of the matter.

Provincial paper

NUDIST NABBED

UNCLOTHED MAN, WHO ADMITS BRANDISHING PISTOL, IS CHARGED WITH CARRYING CONCEALED WEAPON

Providence Journal

Whether the bear was too strong for the cage, or the cage too weak for the bear, may be a subject for investigation.

Daily Mail

WANTED, A Gent's or Lady's Bicycle for a Pure Bred Sable and White Collie.

Lincolnshire paper

FOUND, White Fox-terrier Dog. Apply with name on collar, to 51 Park Rd., Regents Park.

The Daily Telegraph

At Rotterdam a visit to the Zoo helped to form most pleasant recollections of our Dutch friends.

Sportsman

His magnificent try against Wales in the first post-war international at Inverleith will be long remembered by Rugby enthusiasts. He was in his 77th year.

Scots paper

The East Farms Parent Teacher Association will discuss the purchase of a freezer at a meeting tonight at 7.30 at the school. The freezer will be used to keep food hot for the hot lunch programme.

Waterbury Republican

A quarter of an hour before the start Hancock scored an unconverted try for Bath.

Sunday paper

Mr O. R. Wise stated that the whole of the racing fraternity of the Dominion were prepared to stand behind the Minister, provided he stood behind them.

New Zealand paper

Four riders cleared the course of about 800 yds with 14 obstacles, including Miss Richardson (Britain) on Cobler.

Scottish Sunday Express

LOST – between Kneeland St. and Hotel Statler, 2-headed man's snake ring with green and red stones. Reward.

Advert in *Boston Herald*

Pair of ladies found by William Hallet at the Stroudsburg Methodist Church a week ago may be secured by
owner by calling at the church and paying for this ad.

Stroudsburg (Pa.) Record

He was dirty and his eyes, bloodshot from loss of sleep,
were embedded in a fortnight's growth of beard.

Reader's Digest Companion

My teeth were chattering as with a fever-chill, when
they all tumbled out.

The Story Teller

'I was throwing the snowball at some Scouts, not at the
Policeman,' said the boy, pleading not guilty today to a
charge of insulting behaviour.

'Nobody wants to stop you playing snowballs – it is a
grand game – but you must now throw them at policemen,'
said the magistrate, fining him 2s. 6d.

The Star

Although Magritte was born in 1898, there are no paint-
ings of his of that date.

Art and Antiques Weekly

He is here pictured with the caskets containing the il-
luminated scrolls and the Town Clerk, Mr E. W. C.

Blythe News Ashington Post

Between 4 PM and 7 PM, tea and snakes will be
served.

Sign outside an Indian restaurant

Round 3 – Both continued to be cautious in the first minuet, but opened up in the second minuet, when both got in good lefts to the head.

Birmingham paper

Miss T— sang a number of popular ballads while the orchestra played some Strauss waltzes.

Parish magazine

I always scatter crumbs on the waiter to attract the fish.

Angler's Mail

The skeleton was believed to be that of a Saxon worrier.

Express and Echo

RAINCOATS AT LESS THAN COST PRICE
LAST THREE DAYS

Advert in Midlands paper

OUR LOW PRICES ARE THE DIRECT RESULT OF OUR LOWERED PRICE POLICY

Advert in *New York Times*

Mrs A. P. Payne, General Hospital, will not be at home today, owing to her absence from home.

Brisbane Courier

Mr and Miss Dymock have gone for a month to Rotorua for the benefit of Mrs Dymock's health.

New Zealand Mail

C. E. Cox begs to announce that he is now prepared to drill wells for water, gas, oil, cash or old clothes.

Red Deer Advocate

She stood at the foot of the stairs, narrowing her eyes and breathing through her hips.

Saturday Evening Post

Dyke stated in his complaint that the defendant owned a large dog that walked the floor most of the night, held noisy midnight parties, and played a radio so that sleep was impossible.

Australian paper

Hammers: Bulk purchase. Suit home handymen with claw heads.

Advert in *Lancashire Evening Post*

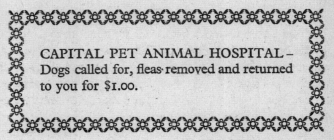

CAPITAL PET ANIMAL HOSPITAL –
Dogs called for, fleas removed and returned
to you for $1.00.

Advert in Washington paper

Mrs Norman, who won a leg of mutton, kindly gave her prize bark and this raised £1.50 for the funds.

Dorset paper

POTTERY STALL – Mrs D— and Miss N—, both useful and ornamental.

Garden fête programme

A committee of ladies, with Mrs Roberts as leader, threw themselves into the tea, which proved a master-piece.

Devon paper

Before Miss Jenkinson concluded the concert by singing 'I'll walk beside you' she was prevented with a bouquet of red roses.

Sussex paper

Confused by the noise of traffic, a cow that probably was experiencing its first taste of city life, got mixed up with vehicles in Milwaukee Avenue yesterday and was struck by a street car. It was so badly injured that Patrolman Stegmiller ended his life with a bullet.

Detroit News

The lad was described as lazy, and when his mother asked him to go to work he threatened to smash her brains out. The case was adjourned for three weeks in order to give the lad another chance.

Manchester paper

Miss Olive Inglis proved to be a young woman wearing a green costume, and a hat trimmed with yellow lace. As there was a previous conviction for a similar offence, she was ordered to find a surety or undergo twenty-one days imprisonment.

Daily Chronicle

For about a year Walton has been manager of the Liv.-Pak Corporation, a firm that ships live lobsters to customers packed in ice.

Boston Post

The bride's bouquet was supplied by Messrs. C—, Arthur Street, and the bridesmaids by Messrs. D—, Shaftesbury Square, Belfast.

Belfast paper

He was born in Ensenada, Mexico, while his parents, both English subjects, were touring the United States.

San Diego Journal

Mr and Mrs John Bowley are the parents of their child, a daughter born at Windsor hospital on August 15th.

Rutland (Vermont) paper

'It is just ridiculous expecting children to travel all that way without seats,' said Mr B. Bateman, one of the Governors and also a railwayman. 'It is something that should not be done even to cattle.'

Yorkshire post

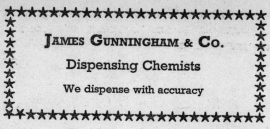

★★★★★★★★★★★★★★★★★★★★★★★★★

JAMES GUNNINGHAM & CO.

Dispensing Chemists

We dispense with accuracy

★★★★★★★★★★★★★★★★★★★★★★★★★

Shop sign

Mrs W. K. Price greeted the guests at the door, and the receiving line was formed by J. Sam Hineon, Mrs J. J. Schuman, R. M. Blaze, Mrs W. G. Helms, Mr & related, the 10 laundries in Charlotte are participants in the special enterprise agree to wash and iron Mrs Spencer, their younger son John and daughter Anna.

Charlotte (N.C.) Observer

Based on a lanolin combination, the suntan oil is readily absorbed by the skin. In the delightful shade of coffee with cream, it will not stain the clothes or the skin.

The results can be so severe as to scar the individual for life.

Houston Post

Edinburgh Women at the Wash-Tub
REMARKABLE FIGURES

Edinburgh Evening News

We have the same eggs for sale that we had last winter. Come and see us.

Pyote (Oklahoma) Clarion

Police anxious to hear from anyone who can give information which may help assailant.

Western Evening Herald (Plymouth)

My son had his arm tattooed in the Navy but now he is getting married he would like it taken off. Is this difficult?

Weekend

But it was decided to pay £50 for the bandstand's demolition. Councillor D. F— was appalling and dangerous.

Yorkshire Post

British Rail have said that they are fully prepared this year if the snow catches them unawares.

Cambridge News

 # UP THE STEPS TO SUNKEN GARDEN

Notice in Canadian park

The bridegroom's mother wore pale grey chiffon with V neck, short sleeves, and skirt having a cascade down the front. With it she wore Harvard University with the Head of the division of chemistry, and returned to Cleveland only a few days ago.

Cleveland paper

Mrs George Earl, who gave birth to a 19-year-old daughter, is reported as getting along fine. A. J. Dill of Farley, who suffered a broken leg in the same accident, is recovering.

Moran Times (Tennessee)

The last he saw of her was as she turned out of a side-street into the main road, tearing up the latter as she went.

Weekly paper

Katherine Riddell was born at the little village of Peasley. Her mother was living there at the time.

Local paper

The stove will stand by itself anywhere. It omits neither smoke nor smell.

Newcastle paper

Special 3 Coarse Lunch 30p.

Notice in Edinburgh café

After a reception the couple left for a honeymoon in Wales. They wore green dresses trimmed with yellow daisies.

Havering Recorder

Easter matinee 10 AM Saturday. Every child laying egg in usher's hand will be admitted free!

Notice outside Birmingham cinema

FULL-TIME or part-time Ladies' Hairstylist required – Apply . . . . must hold heavy goods licence.

Leamington Spa Morning News

White satin wedding dress, 40″ bust with train, separate ribbon lace bodice, headdress, veil, BBC and ITV aerial.

Dean Forest Guardian

Externally the design is modern, and internally the treatment is somewhat severe, as is usual in a hospital.

The Daily Telegraph

He returned in a few minutes and announced the visitor in faultless English – 'Signor Tillizani.'

Short story

Feed your dog as you would feed your friend. Give him Blank's dog biscuits.

Advert in Essex paper

Fortunately for the workman the glass fell per-pendicularly, for had it fallen vertically the accident in all probability would have proved serious.

Taranaki Daily News

It is not considered polite to tear bits off your beard and put them in your soup.

Etiquette book

The Lomas Fire Brigade was soon on the scene and helped by members of the railway personnel were able to reduce the two carriages to a smouldering heap.

Buenos Aires Herald

Mrs Collins says she is not bothered that the baby did not turn out to be a girl, as she half expected.

New Zealand Weekly

She cried out in agony. And at that instant she heard a horse whisper behind her.

Indian paper

MISSING, part-Persian cat, brown and orange. Finder rewarded, dead or alive.

Advert in Yorks paper

GOOD HORSE, complete with saddle and bridle, 6 volt battery, pistons, connecting rods, etc.

Advert in *Nigerian Times*

It's a good idea, before you give your hair its nightly brushing, to begin the operation with a brick massage to loosen your scalp and to start the circulation of the blood.

Ann Arbor (Michigan) News

Anne crept cautiously up the stairs and knocked timidly at the door with the jelly.

From a novel

An item which was deservedly appreciated and encored was Chopin's Polonaise 'Sea Miner'.

Wexford Free Press

It was heard under excellent conditions, Miss Wayne and Mr Charles were obviously at home and in complete sympathy with their parts, the mooing duet being snug with the deepest feeling and dramatic fervour.

Yorkshire Evening News

Twenty-two members were present at the meeting of the R.L.D.S. Church held at the home of Mrs Edith Marchfield last evening. Mrs Ruth Bayliss and Monica Hotton sung a duet, The Lord Knows Why.

Attleboro (Massachusetts) Sun

Detectives were investigating a break-in at the Knightsbridge flat of property dealer Mr S. J. L—. The raiders are believed to have taken only a small amount of property.

Evening Standard

The dispute too, is over redundancy – and scattered showers. Drizzle fitters and a foreman electrician.

Evening News (Dublin)

Steel wool toilet rolls 2½p each.

Advert in Stoke-on-Trent hardware shop

A searing pain shot across my throat. I fell to the ground writhing. A pack of dogs ran out to whelp round me.

Sunday Post (Glasgow)

Mr Michael K— Q.C. and Mr Sydney T— Q.C. ate the two other members of the panel.

Express and Star (Wolverhampton)

The bride wore an ivory georgette dress with a Brussels net veil. The bridegroom wore the DSO.

South London paper

The marriage of Miss Anna Bloch and Mr Willis Dashwood, which was announced in this paper a few weeks ago, was a mistake and we wish to correct.

Colorado paper

Hugh and Ruth went to country high-school together with Kansas, and their marriage will stop a romance begun between them there.

West Virginia paper

A huge collar of white fox fur successfully concealed the greater part of Mrs David T—'s face.

Gossip column

Mr and Mrs Raymond Tibbetts, 627 Main Street, are the parents of a son named Teddy Roy, born Sunday at Dukes Hospital to Mr and Mrs Charles Hilleman of 526 East Canal Street.

Logansport (Indiana) *Press*

It was a hot day and the effect of cooked fish left standing for an unknown time on the tummy of a homewardbound excursionist was not pleasant to contemplate.

Daily Mail

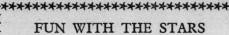

FUN WITH THE STARS

Today for Everybody. Your own judgement may be much better than that of other people during the initial stages of the day.

Daily Express

This work will afford protection from the smell which, when the wind is in the east, has caused ships to break away from their moorings, often parting large hawsers.

Commercial weekly

The Forton Street bridge was repaired following its collapse a number of months ago. New end-plates that held a truss were installed and the bridge is in about the same condition it was prior to its collapse in the fall.

Wisconsin paper

Dr Daly, discussing the request for an inquiry, said he might make a foul statement later.

Bermuda paper

Please suggest a cold fish dish to be made from leftover chicken.

Woman's Way (Dublin)

The man who took the green jacket is said to be in his late 20s . . . thick set, with a light blue beard.

Evening News (Bolton)

PATIENTS LOCKED UP

Only skeleton staff as strike
of nurses becomes critical.

Dublin Evening Herald

! You get one ton of Tomato Paste FREE with **!**
every packet of Blank's Spaghetti and Macaroni.

Advert in *Daily Mail* (Sierra Leone)

Sincere sympathy is expressed to all who supported the Film Show, which raised £3 for church funds.

Torrington Deanery Magazine

Receptionist with some experience of handling cosh under busy customer conditions required.

Evening Times (Glasgow)

Black lace-up PLIMSOLLS available in all colours.

Barnsley Chronicle and South Yorkshire News

In our last week's issue we announced the birth of a son to Mr and Mrs Gilbert Parkinson. We regret any annoyance that this may have caused.

Indian paper

This picture shows the 'Blizzard Baby' who was born in a hospital parking lot unnoticed by her father and mother, who collapsed as she stepped from an automobile.

American weekly

Mr and Mrs A. P. Hageman are rejoicing over the arrival of a mafwpy cmfwyp emfwpy cmfwpp doing nicely.

Florida paper

Miss Dorothy Morrison, who was injured by a fall from a horse last week, is in St Joseph's Hospital and covered sufficiently to see her friends.

Morristown (N.D.) News

Twelve shoppers on a crowded Brooklyn thoroughfare were injured yesterday . . . when a 65-year-old woman lost control of her car, mounted the curb and ran for forty feet among pedestrians on the sidewalk.

New York paper

To avoid overloading of a boat, have the weight evenly distributed.

American do-it-yourself journal

Roughly chop the walnuts. Mix the celery, apples and walnuts into the salad cream or mayonnaise and add salt and pepper to taste. Turn the mixture into a polythene box.

Recipe in *Q. Performance* (Duckhams Oils)

If the surface is rough, give it two goats.

Practical Householder

The Colonel scurried up a tree while the dog closed with the bear and killed him with four well-placed bullets.

Pennsylvania paper

Bernard Colodney of 754 Mamaroneck Avenue was given a summons yesterday for permitting a dog to run at large after it was struck and killed in front of his address by a car.

White-Plains Reporter-Dispatch

Stop and think for a moment. Many people are all run down, tired out and hardly able to drag about – don't know what's the matter with them. The answer, of course, is Blank's Cod Liver Extract, the great tissue builder.

Advert in *Lahore Civil and Military Gazette*

'You can fool some of the people all the time, and all the people some of the time, but you can't fool all the people all the time.' This is the idea on which our business has been built up.

Advert in *Johannesburg Daily Mail*

TO CLEAR – £1 each, 5 new 4-barrel Repeating Pistols 22 bore. Cannot repeat.

Advert in Sussex paper

Pierre fingered one of his ears caressingly and looked thoughtfully at the other.

Serial in weekly paper

Exasperated, Sandro drew his dagger and struck straight at Louise's heart; she died on the spot.
Read the article by Gaston Benac in the sporting section.

France-soir

As he uttered the all-important word he dropped his voice, but she just managed to catch it.

Short story in evening paper

He put the melting honey-coloured fruit on her plate and got out a silk handkerchief. She began to eat it thoughtfully.

Serial in daily paper

Woofey, the rough-haired terrier belonging to Mrs Perkins of Boundary Road, wags his tail at the shop doorway until Mr Bert Williams, who keeps the shop for his father, picks up the meat in his mouth and takes it home.

Norfolk paper

Position as daily help wanted by respectable woman (Sundays excepted).

Scots paper

If they could save children from dying before the age of one there was a better prospect of them reaching to adolescence.

South London paper

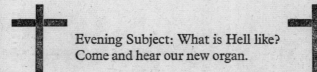

Evening Subject: What is Hell like?
Come and hear our new organ.

Notice board at Cumberland church

Mr and Mrs Bond of Duke Hill are the parents of any infant daughter born Thursday.

Illinois paper

To prevent a little girl's hair slide from constantly slipping, put an elastic band or a piece of bicycle valve tubing round the under arm, opposite the teeth.

Woman's Illustrated

Undoubtedly the club is the place for a bachelor. It is not right, however, for a married man to pass the evenings away from home while his poor wife sadly rocks the cradle with one foot and wipes away the tears with the other.

Church sermon

Have plenty of orangs in the house. They can be relied on to keep the doctor away.

Woman's paper

The service ended with the singing of the good old hymn: 'All police that on earth do dwell.'

Canadian paper

The happy pair then left for Scotland by car. The parents were numerous and costly.

Local paper

THIS APPLIANCE
WILL REDUCE
YOUR HIPS, OR BUST

Advert in People's Home Journal

The gutted carcase of a deer was found yesterday afternoon near Fonthill Road. While investigating this, State Trooper Howard Johnson was bitten on the left arm by a dog owned by Miss Ann Lacko of Fonthill Road.

Police at the local sub-station said the dog would be let loose and Johnson tied up for ten days.

New Jersey paper

BUNGALOW FOR SALE, consisting of valuable window sashes, corrugated iron roof.

Irish Times

I did not see Mr M— at the Antique Dealer's Fair last week, and later I heard that he has retired from the business and is faking things quietly at home.

Gossip column

The Chairman said defendant would be fined £2 and his licence endorsed. If he did not mind he would be disqualified from driving altogether.

Police Court News

The show was put on by the Da Silva Puppet Company which travels round Britain once in the afternoon and again in the early evening.

Ormskirk Advertiser

We regret to state that Mr M— who is seriously indisposed at his residence, showed slight signs of improvement yesterday.

West Indian paper

Miss S— sang the first verse and then the audience all sank together.

Local paper

In printing yesterday the name of one of the musical comedies which the Bandmaster Company is presenting next week as The Grill in the Train, what our compositor meant to set was, of course, the Girl in the Drain.

South China Morning Post

At the studios, a tiny baby was needed for a scene in The Enemy. The call came to Peggy C—, studio nurse. 'Please have a baby by eight o'clock tomorrow morning.'

Photoplay

Before placing your orders in the usual channel for the coming term, we should like you to be thoroughly convinced that our services can be dispensed with advantageously.

Tradesman's circular

. . . but the petition of Stanley Zwier, American civic worker, who was found this morning shoved under the door of the City Manager's office, will be accepted.

New Jersey paper

The library will be closed five minutes before closing time.

Notice in Munich public library

The Hon. Treasurer (Mr Hodgson) stated that he was willing to carry on in his office until he had to move from the town, which might be at any time (applause).

Andover Advertiser

John Sewell, a public health department inspector, said he visited the potted meat manufacturer and found it was prepared by chopping tinned boiled beef to which spices, gelatine, and boiling water were added. The mixture was made up in ten pound notes.

Daily paper

We charge low prices of admission but they are recognized by our regular visitors as being consistent with the quality of the films screened.

Singapore Free Press

Marjorie would often take her eyes from the deck and cast them far out to sea.

Short story

There was no damage to the truck, but the two front fenders, headlight, bumper-guard, and girl of Fitzgerald's car were damaged.

Mamaroneck (New York) *Times*

'Is the photographer there yet? cover the murder yet?'

'The murder?'

Winslow made an automatic dash for his camera, called us, called the no murder. Finally the story came out. Parties unnamed had just wanted to see how excited they could get Winslow.

We couldn't check this story into her henhouse and found no near Leesburg house-wife but it just as good anyhow.

'If only I had an egg,' she lamented to herself, probably hen walked over to her, stopped.

At that very moment, an old thinking about breakfast, deposited a single egg on the floor at her feet and walked off.

'How's that for service?'

Leesburg (Virginia) *Loudoun News*

Man critical after bus backs into him

Middletown (Conn.) *Press*

He had killed Nana once and she had ignored it. Too inexperienced perhaps to make anything of it.

Dallas Times-Herald

Lassalle fell in love in a few moments, carried the woman of his choice down exactly three flights of stairs, and then, as though his intellect had interfered to dampen his emotions, he let the whole matter drop.

From *Genius and Character* by Emil Ludwig

Six minutes later Blackpool went further ahead, when Matthews saw his left foot curl into the net off a post.

Football report

At the start of the race Yale went out in front, rowing at a terrific clip above 40. It had half a mile lead after the first quarter mile.

New York Times

It is necessary for technical reasons that these warheads should be stored with the top at the bottom, and the bottom at the top. In order that there may be no doubt as to which is the top and which is the bottom for storage purposes, it will be seen that the bottom of each head has been plainly labelled with the word TOP.

Admiralty instruction

'Put soap on the runners of the bureau drawers instead of jerking them in and out until they fall apart,' advises John Litwinko.

'If that doesn't help, take the the Methodist Episcopal Church.'

Philadelphia Evening Bulletin

I have been sitting at the window making note of the number of buses, and the contents of passengers.

Letter in Hampstead paper

Mrs Frank Brundage received a long-distance message on Saturday evening informing her of the birth of a baby son, born Saturday afternoon at their home in St Paul. The baby weighed 8 lb 9 oz.

Iowa paper

Mr and Mrs Benny Croset announce the birth of a little son which arrived on the 5.15 last Thursday.

West Union (Oregon) *People's Defender*

Dr Linus Pauling a Nobel Prize winner claims that vitamin C prevents clouds.

Ceylon Observer

It is hoped that large numbers of students, parents and teachers will attend the lecture to which there is no admission.

Western People

Following the fire in the work in York Hill, planning applications to rebuild the factory were refused, so that nasty repairs had to suffice.

West Essex Gazette

FOR SALE – A small, large house in St. George's Hill, conveniently placed.

Surrey Herald

With the Saint (Roger Moore) on ATV and Paul Temple (Francis Matthews) on BBC 1 – bath at 8 PM of course – there's a difficult choice...

Leicester Mercury

★ Special offer Moulinex Marvel Mixer – it beats, whips, mixes and creams with no effect at all.

Irish Times

Moota Restaurant and Motel .... Restaurant and supper licence. Specialities: Roast Proprietors: Mr I. H. E—.

Lakescene

The shape of a child's mouth can be ruined by a rubber tummy.

Advert in *Wandsworth Borough News*

If you have enjoyed this PICCOLO Book, you may like to choose your next book from the titles listed on the following pages.

Puzzles and Games

True Adventures and Picture Histories

Piccolo Book Selection

These and other PICCOLO Books are obtainable from all booksellers and newsagents. If you have any difficulty please send purchase price plus 7p postage to PO Box 11, Falmouth, Cornwall.

While every effort is made to keep prices low, it is sometimes necessary to increase prices at short notice. PAN Books reserve the right to show new retail prices on covers which may differ from those advertised in the text or elsewhere.

KV-513-367

'You have humiliated me, Colonel,' he said
quietly. 'You have caused me to lose the trust
of the people for whom I have worked for many
years. You have brought about the death of one
of our most valued agents: Fraulein Eklund, for
whom the younger Von Regen felt a special
affection. Now his father, the count, is on his
way here to see for himself that you will no
longer be a problem. It humiliates me even
further that he feels required to do this.'
'You better tell your count all you've got is one
man,' I grunted. 'The others will keep going.
They don't need me.'